FAQ
TEEN LIFE™

FREQUENTLY ASKED QUESTIONS ABOUT

Foster Care

Annie Leah
Sommers

ROSEN
PUBLISHING®

New York

To Mary Walker

Published in 2010 by The Rosen Publishing Group, Inc.
29 East 21st Street, New York, NY 10010

Library of Congress Cataloging-in-Publication Data

Sommers, Annie Leah, 1968–
Frequently asked questions about foster care / Annie Leah Sommers.
    p. cm.—(FAQ: teen life)
Includes bibliographical references and index.
ISBN 978-1-4358-3546-7 (library binding)
1. Foster home care. 2. Foster children. 3. Questions and answers. I. Title.
HV873.S67 2010
362.73'3—dc22

                                                2009014418

Manufactured in Malaysia

CPSIA Compliance Information: Batch #TWW10YA: For Further Information contact Rosen Publishing, New York, New York at 1-800-237-9932

Contents

Chapter one

WHAT IS FOSTER CARE?

In the United States, there are approximately six hundred thousand young people who are living in the foster care system. At times, it can be a complex system that may seem overwhelming. However, knowing how foster care works, what to expect, and how other teens in foster care cope can be extremely helpful.

In the United States, the Department of Social Services (DSS) is the government agency in charge of the foster care system. The goal of foster care is to provide children in need of a better home life with a safe and welcoming environment among responsible and caring adults. Foster care children can range in age from newborn to twenty-one years old. What they all have in common is that they live in a home other than that of their birth parents'.

There are many reasons children might not be able to live at home. In some cases, birth parents are not able to care for their children. They may be struggling financially or may be extremely ill. Other children may suffer from the instability caused by parents with a substance abuse problem. In other cases, youth are removed from their parents' care when their home environment becomes violent or dangerous.

Children whose parents are physically or mentally abusive are often candidates for foster care. Tragically, there are also cases in which parents suffer from illness or sometimes death and children are left alone, often without any close relatives that can take care of them. No matter what the reason, all teens in foster care will likely experience some of the same challenges and share some of the same feelings.

How Foster Care Works

Foster care can be overwhelming, especially because as a foster youth, you may feel very alone. After all, for whatever reason, you're not able to rely upon or turn to your birth parents. And suddenly you're leaving behind things that are familiar to you to go somewhere completely unknown where you'll be among strangers. Although it can be a big relief to get away from a painful or even dangerous home situation, the transition to a new home can be scary.

Although you may feel alone, try to remember that you're not. A lot of other teens are in the same boat as you. There are also many adults who have spent a lifetime working and living with foster children who are ready to help you navigate the child welfare system. A really useful way to find out more about being

Terry Ross, age seventeen, holds Kyboo the dog while smiling in a photo with his soon to be adopted family in Sacramento, California. He is going to be adopted one week before he turns eighteen.

Sometimes, foster teens are placed in residential treatment centers (RTC). These are group homes where young people live in a structured, campus-like environment while going to school. RTCs have staff that are specially trained to care for foster teens with specific needs. Examples include group homes for pregnant teens where young women learn how to become good mothers while getting the prenatal care they require. It could also be a home where youth with learning disabilities live and receive special care and education. What's good about these living situations is that you'll be with other teenagers who share the same to care for their children. They may be struggling financially or may be extremely ill. Other children may suffer from the instability caused by parents with a substance abuse problem. In other cases, youth are removed from their parents' care when their home environment becomes violent or dangerous.

Children whose parents are physically or mentally abusive are often candidates for foster care. Tragically, there are also cases in which parents suffer from illness or sometimes death and children are left alone, often without any close relatives that can take care of them. No matter what the reason, all teens in foster care will likely experience some of the same challenges and share some of the same feelings.

How Foster Care Works

Foster care can be overwhelming, especially because as a foster youth, you may feel very alone. After all, for whatever reason, you're not able to rely upon or turn to your birth parents. And suddenly you're leaving behind things that are familiar to you to go somewhere completely unknown where you'll be among strangers. Although it can be a big relief to get away from a painful or even dangerous home situation, the transition to a new home can be scary.

Although you may feel alone, try to remember that you're not. A lot of other teens are in the same boat as you. There are also many adults who have spent a lifetime working and living with foster children who are ready to help you navigate the child welfare system. A really useful way to find out more about being

Teri LaCourse and her father Pat LaCourse tie a blue ribbon on a tree for National Foster Care Month. Each ribbon placed on the tree represents a foster child in the area.

in foster care is by asking questions and learning from others, especially from other teens who are or have been in foster care. Just as important as talking with other children is speaking with adults who can help you understand the basics of the foster care system. Armed with this knowledge, you will be equipped to help yourself get the best care possible. As a result of being informed, you'll feel less scared, stressed, and confused and will have realistic expectations about foster care. More important, you'll be more in charge of your own life and your future.

Where Will I Live?

If you are not able to live with your birth parents, how do you end up with a foster family? Placing you with a foster family is the responsibility of the government. Depending upon the state in which you live, the government agency in charge may be called Child Protective Services, the Department of Social Services, or the Department of Children and Family Care Services. Sometimes, government agencies work with private agencies. In some states, the private agency may be referred to as a contract agency, a provider agency, or simply "the agency." No matter what it's called, the goal will always be the same: to find you a home.

Being placed in a foster home means you'll be taken care of by people who have received training on how to be foster parents. Such training ensures that these caregivers can provide you with a safe and nurturing home environment. It also helps make foster parents aware of the issues and emotional situations foster teens may be facing.

In general, living with a foster family involves moving into a family's house or apartment where, along with your foster parents, you'll likely be living with the foster parents' own birth children and, in some cases, other foster youth as well. However, when possible, children may be placed with another family member, such as an older sibling (over the age of twenty-one), a grandparent, a cousin, or an aunt or uncle. This type of living situation is often referred to as kinship care. If neither living with a foster family nor other relatives is possible, there are other options.

Terry Ross, age seventeen, holds Kyboo the dog while smiling in a photo with his soon to be adopted family in Sacramento, California. He is going to be adopted one week before he turns eighteen.

Sometimes, foster teens are placed in residential treatment centers (RTC). These are group homes where young people live in a structured, campus-like environment while going to school. RTCs have staff that are specially trained to care for foster teens with specific needs. Examples include group homes for pregnant teens where young women learn how to become good mothers while getting the prenatal care they require. It could also be a home where youth with learning disabilities live and receive special care and education. What's good about these living situations is that you'll be with other teenagers who share the same problems and experiences as you. Living together can be a great learning experience.

Some foster youth may initially find themselves in an emergency shelter. If your family household becomes so dangerous that your health or even your life is in danger, immediate action is necessary. A teenager may be taken from his or her home and placed in an emergency shelter for a short period of time until a more permanent care solution can be found. Teens might also be temporarily placed in such a shelter if they are experiencing serious problems with their foster family.

The average length of stay in foster care is a little more than two years. The hope is that during this time, birth parents will get help or counseling that will ultimately improve family life and make it safe for you to return home. The reality is that sometimes it can take longer for this to happen. In such instances, it is quite likely that you will end up moving at least once. The average teenager in foster care lives in two to five different homes over a period of two and a half years. Some teens end up moving three or four times in a year.

Constant upheavals and change can seem overwhelming. After all, you've probably already got your hands full just dealing with high school and all the normal concerns that come with simply being a teenager. Remember that these are normal feelings.

Where Can I Find Help?

Within the foster care system, each individual case involves many people. Often, it can be tough to keep track of all these

Vermont Department of Social and Rehabilitative Services Commissioner William Young *(left)*, carefully listens while a group of foster teens discuss issues that they face while in state custody.

professionals and what their jobs are. Talking to your case-worker and law guardian is really important since they understand how the whole system works and can usually address any issues you may have.

However, you can also take the initiative by doing some research on your own. You can find out tons of really useful things about what it's like to be in foster care by reading books like this or checking out Web sites, chat forums, and blogs on the Internet that are specifically geared to foster teens. Many associations and agencies that specialize in foster care have lots of literature and usually host Web sites. Your local library is another really good source. You'll find a lot of information on where to look at the back of this book. There is help available, you just have to remember to ask for it.

Ten Great Questions to Ask a Foster Care Specialist

1 Who will look after me?

2 Where will I live?

3 Can I see my birth parents?

4 When can I go back home?

5 Do I have to go to court?

6 Who can I talk to if I have problems?

7 How many times do I have to move?

8 Can my brother or sisters get placed with me?

9 Do other teens in foster care feel the same way I do?

10 Will I have to change schools?

chapter two

HOW DO I ADJUST TO MY NEW HOME?

No matter what type of foster home you are going to be living in, it's your caseworker's job to help you settle in and make any adjustments. As such, it's definitely a smart idea to understand what he or she does.

Your caseworker:

- Knows and will protect your rights
- Provides you with information such as whom you will be living with and where
- Visits you and your caregivers regularly to ensure that everything is all right
- Is responsible for transferring records from your old school to a new one, in the case you have to move
- Is the person most involved in helping you make plans for your future

During a training session at Lawrenceville, New Jersey, New Jersey state Division of Youth and Family Services caseworker trainee Joseph Camiolo, far right, asks questions.

Because your caseworker is so important, make sure that you have his or her most current contact information—full name, phone number, and e-mail address. This way you can be in touch immediately if you have questions or problems. It's also useful to ask for the contact information of your case-worker's supervisor, whom you can contact if you can't reach your caseworker or in the event you are having difficulties with him or her. A lot of foster children are in the dark as to who their caseworkers actually work for. In most situations, they may work for a private foster care agency in conjunction with the local Department of Social Services, but some work directly with the DSS. The best way to find out is to ask.

Settling in After a Move

When your caseworker takes you to your new foster home, it may take some time to get settled in. Initially, you'll be introduced to your foster parents. If you're in a group home, you'll meet the staff who will be in charge of your care. These first encounters can be pretty nerve-wracking. You may find you have knots in your stomach and feel slightly anxious or afraid. Don't worry—this is a perfectly normal reaction. In fact, it's to be expected, and your caseworker will do whatever possible to help you feel more at ease.

Hopefully this transition will be as smooth as possible and you will be prepared in advance. However, sometimes emergency situations occur when teens need to be moved suddenly. Under such circumstances, you may find yourself rushing to pack up your belongings and taking leave of your family home, perhaps in the midst of a lot of conflict. This can be really upsetting, especially if when you left the situation between you and your birth parents was pretty ugly. As difficult as the sudden departure may seem, try to take comfort in the fact that you will soon be settled in a calmer environment that is less stressful and harmful to you, where you're surrounded by people concerned with your well-being.

After meeting your caregivers, you'll want to inspect the space in which you'll be living and find out where you'll be sleeping. You may end up with your own room or sharing a room with biological children of your foster parents or other foster children. Before your caseworker leaves, he or she will check to make sure that your space is adequate for you. Ask your caregiver where you can store your belongings and start unpacking as soon as possible. This will ease the transition and help make you feel more at home. A space feels more like your home once you have filled it up and decorated it with your belongings.

Adjusting to Your New Home

So that you know from the beginning how things work around your new home, it's a good idea to ask questions about how the household runs so that you'll have a clear sense of what your responsibilities are.

What Are the Rules Here?

Start off by asking your caregiver or a staff member of a group facility about any house rules. Are there certain hours when you can or can't watch television or use the phone or Internet? How are household chores divided up? Is there a time that you're expected to be home at night?

In a group home or residential treatment center, you'll want to know what times meals are served, when you can make phone calls, and if there's a computer you can use. There is

Keeping a journal or a diary is an excellent way for youth in foster care to keep track of their own feelings as well as note down useful information that's easy to access.

probably a list of rules already created. Ask to see it and make a copy for your personal reference. In a private foster care home where the rules are up to the individual foster parents, ask up front and maybe write down specifics in a notebook or journal. Although foster parents will have their own rules—which may already apply to their own children or other foster children living under their roof—there is usually room to negotiate as you get to know each other.

Some rules to ask about include the following:

- Am I able to go to a friend's house after school?
  (You may need to get permission in advance or your foster parent may say it's fine for you to call once you are there. The same rule may apply to inviting a friend over after school; it's best to check in advance.)
- What if I want to play a sport at school or attend a high school football game?
  (In some states, if you want to try out for the team, you may need to get permission from your caseworker and/or your foster parent. To be safe, check with your caseworker, who will have the most up-to-date requirements)
- Do I have a curfew?
- Am I allowed to get a part-time job?
- Can I visit a friend, relative, or birth parent who lives out of state?
  (For most out-of-area visits, you will need to get permission from your caseworker since he or she is

responsible for you in the county you live in regardless of placement.)

- How can I take part in the same religious services I attended before?
- Can I drive the family car?

As a new member of the household, it's natural that you'll be asked by your foster parents or caregivers to do some chores around the house, such as setting the table, taking out garbage, or folding laundry. Although you may not have done them before, and they may seem boring, doing household chores is a good way to gain skills and a sense of responsibility. Pitching in will also make you feel more like part of the family or group. Keep in mind: you should not expect to be paid for this kind of work in a foster home or facility. It is all a part of living in a home with others. If you feel that you are being asked to do too much, if you think you are being treated unfairly, or if you are being threatened in any way, contact your caseworker immediately.

How Do Other Teens React?

It can be helpful—and comforting—to talk to other foster teens. They can give you precious insight into what you can expect while you're in foster care. You may feel overwhelmed by a lot of intense feelings. Knowing that other children have gone through similar situations and experienced the same emotions can be reassuring.

Doing chores such as laundry can actually help you feel more like you're a part of the family. At the same time, you'll get a chance to learn some new skills.

Is It Normal to Feel Confused?

According to a therapist and grief specialist at the Center for Adoption Support and Education, teens who experience parental loss are very likely to be dealing with feelings of anger, confusion, sadness, fear, guilt, and numbness. Experiencing one or even all of these emotions is very normal.

As mentioned earlier, it may take you a while to process the immense changes that have happened to you, especially if the period prior to your leaving home was filled with conflict. Don't expect to understand everything all at once. It can take a while to digest things. The best thing you can do, however, is to try not to deny or hide your feelings. You may think that because you're a young "adult," you're old enough and tough enough to deal with complex situations on your own, without any help. But the truth is, most foster teens live through some pretty tough times that many adults would have difficulty dealing with on their own. So open up to those around you, and if you find yourself feeling really down, hopeless, sad, or guilty, find someone you can talk to.

For teens who have experienced multiple placements, the emotional reaction to yet another move can be numbness. Unfortunately, some teens may have already had five or even ten or fifteen placements. This translates into a revolving door of new and different schools, neighborhoods, friends, and care-givers and/or foster families. It may seem as though every time you begin to get settled, you're being uprooted again.

A very common response to so much displacement is to shut down emotionally, even to the point where you tell your

Being in foster care can often mean having to deal with an awful lot of changes—all of these things can lead to a complicated mix of emotions.

caseworker, "No way, I'm not moving again." Another common reaction is to get angry and resentful. Some teens get so frustrated by what they sense as lack of control over their lives that they act out aggressively, seeing this as a way of rebelling against a situation in which they feel they have no control. Remember that it takes a lot of energy to create new connections, so don't get discouraged.

While some teens may act out, others may get to the point where they want to drop out—just give up and leave the system. Although this may be a natural impulse, the truth is that foster teens who react by running away and being declared AWOL (absent without leave) end up making things much more complicated for themselves. Instead of solving any problems, you could miss out on getting a good placement that could really improve your situation.

Being Misunderstood

Unfortunately, there are some cases where teenagers' complex and seemingly contradictory emotions lead too quickly (and unfairly) to them being judged as uncooperative or problematic. As a result, you may find yourself being treated as a "difficult case." Studies of teenagers in the foster care system show that in situations where communication is limited, foster youth are often misunderstood. Caseworkers, as well as caregivers and teachers, will witness certain types of behavior and conclude that the youth in question is simply being a troublemaker. There are even cases when a youth's behavior has been referred to mistakenly as a learning disability or a mental health issue.

While such reactions are certainly unfair, no matter how hard it is to convince yourself otherwise, try to realize that giving up trying to be understood is not the way to go. If you feel really lost and that your whole universe is collapsing, instead of shutting down or lashing out, make an effort to speak up and express your feelings to your caseworker, foster parents or caregivers, or another adult you trust and respect, such as a guidance counselor, teacher, coach, or even the parent of a friend. Hard as it may be, sometimes, speaking up and expressing yourself is all that you can do. And it can be enough to make a difference.

Myths and Facts

Myth

You'll never be successful in your career if you end up in foster care.

Fact: ➡ Foster care is a situation, not an identity. It doesn't have to hold you back. Examples of famous people who were in foster care include Ice-T, John Lennon, and Babe Ruth.

Myth

Foster youth never get adopted because there are not enough adults who want them.

Fact: ➡ According to a National Adoption Attitudes Survey, four out of ten American adults have considered adopting a foster care child.

Myth

Some adults get paid for taking in foster children.

Fact: ➡ Foster parents receive an allowance or stipend from the agency that must go toward providing the foster child with food and shelter.

WHAT ARE
MY RIGHTS?

As a teenager in the foster care system, you may feel that decisions about your care are made without a lot of input from you. Knowing your rights can help you feel like you have more control. Being in foster care can be quite challenging in many ways, but increasingly, youth and adult partners are working together in their home states to improve the child welfare system.

According to many professionals in the field, young people in foster care are not aware of all the legislation that has been put in place to help protect them because they aren't always told about their rights. Moreover, sometimes they are so busy adjusting to their new lives that they just don't think about asking.

If you're in foster care right now, take some time to sit down and think about any questions you might have about your rights. Do you have a clear sense of what's expected of you at your new home? Do you understand what goes on at court? Do you have an idea of what will happen in the future? Being well informed is especially vital if you are an older teen because you'll need to prepare for leaving or aging out of the system. Knowing what the system will do for you helps you to be better equipped to have a say in both your day-to-day life and in preparing for your future. And you don't need to have a degree in law or social work to understand what it's all about.

What Is Family Court?

First of all, it's important to have an understanding of how the system works. As a foster teen, you've probably heard about family court. Something you're used to seeing on a nightly television program may seem intimidating in real life. Or maybe you haven't really thought about court at all. Whatever the case, it is good to know that family court was created to resolve problems faced by youth and their families. As a teen in the foster care system, the role of family court is to assist and protect you. This is where discussions about your rights will take place, and it's here that the most important decisions about your placement, care, and future will be debated and decided upon.

Some Basics

Once a new foster care placement is confirmed, you will start going to regular hearings at family court to monitor your care.

A children's attorney talks to her client in court at the William Ridgeway Family Relations courthouse in Sacramento, California. It is important to attend all court hearings.

These meetings are supposed to take place every six months, and it's important to make it to all hearings. After all, you're the star of the show. If you've been in care for a while and you haven't been to a hearing, contact your caseworker immediately and ask when the next meeting is.

There are a lot of people involved in your case, and it's good to have a sense of who you'll be dealing with in court. As soon you as you enter the foster care system, the Department of Social Services (or state equivalent) has custody of you. This means that they are in charge of your care. The DSS is represented by your caseworker, who is your most important contact in the system. Often, the government agency will work with a private agency. In this case, you'll have a caseworker from the private agency who communicates with a government caseworker. You will also have a lawyer who will represent you in court. It's important to know that you have the right to speak with your lawyer whenever you need to. Everything that you say to your lawyer remains strictly confidential. In fact, your lawyer should ask for your permission if things you've said in confidence are going to be passed on to others.

You, your caseworker(s), and your lawyer will meet in family court. These meetings will most probably occur during the day and will often conflict with your classes at school. However, since you have a legal right to attend the meetings, your teacher must excuse you from class. Your caseworker will speak with your teachers so that you have permission to leave school. Don't forget to ask your teachers for any missed assignments when you are back in class.

Day-to-Day Living

You also have a lot of rights in terms of how you live and what kind of a home situation you can expect. How you feel in the physical space in which you live has a big impact on your mood. Regardless of whether you'll be there for a few weeks or several years, feeling comfortable in your home is essential. It doesn't matter whether you end up in a large apartment building, a single-family home, a government-subsidized housing project, or a dorm-like room in a group home, there

Many foster care youths share their bedrooms with the children of the families that adopt them.

are aspects of home life that you should always be able to count on.

Where Do I Sleep?

In terms of foster care homes, there are certain rules that apply to all living situations (although depending on the state you live in, there will be some variation in the law). It's good to be aware of the following:

- In a private home, you are entitled to sleep in a proper bedroom; no beds are allowed in any unfinished space, especially in an unfurnished attic or basement.

- Anyone eighteen years of age or older should not be sharing a room with a foster youth over the age of three.
- In group homes, there should always be separate sleeping facilities for youth of the opposite sex.
- Adult caregivers should sleep in separate rooms.
- You should have good natural light and ventilation, with at least one window that opens to the outside.

Speak to your caseworker if you are not comfortable in your room or if you are not given an adequate place to sleep.

What About My Belongings?

You may be familiar with the term "right to privacy." This means that according to the law, you are allowed to have some private space for yourself and your belongings. In any foster home setting, you should be given your own space where you can store your possessions—clothing, books, photos, journal, or diary—safely and securely. No one should have access to your possessions.

What If I Need New Clothes?

Some teenagers enter the foster care system with nothing but the clothes on their backs at the time of being transferred from their birth homes to placement. At other times, due to poorly addressed mail, inaccurate or incomplete forwarding addresses, carelessness, or even theft, you may lose some items of clothing.

While it's an inconvenience and upsetting to lose things, try to feel some degree of relief in knowing that you will be receiving a clothing allowance. This will most probably come from your caseworker at the local Department of Social Services. It's best to ask your caseworker how this allowance is received.

Typically, foster children are given payments of about $200 every three months. This can stretch pretty far if you shop carefully. Aside from this sum, you are also entitled to receive a special clothing allowance to cover any additional items you need for dressing up, religious ceremonies, proms, or other school events. This also includes things you may need because of the climate where you live, such as a warm winter jacket. Keep in mind that this money is different from the stipend your foster family receives from the government. That money helps your new family pay for your food and lodging.

Health Care and Hygiene

No matter what type of home you are placed in, you have the right to have access to soap, a toothbrush, toothpaste, and a towel. You have a right to be clean and take a shower or bath every day. As a youth in foster care, you have a right to receive free health care. Even if you are a minor (under age eighteen), you are able to access health care on your own, without having to get permission from an adult. Do be aware that there is some variation depending on the state you live in. However, as long as you are clear about the benefits and potential risk involved, you

In a long awaited moment, Chad Svenby, age twenty-three, embraces his birth mother, Darla Allgood, at Anchorage International Airport in Alaska.

have access to health care without needing consent from an adult for the following:

- Emergency health care
- Certain alcohol and drug abuse services
- Certain mental health services
- Testing for HIV and care for STDs (sexually transmitted diseases)

In other cases, your foster parent or caseworker may need to give consent.

Neither you nor your family should be asked to pay for these services. The cost will be covered by Medicaid or another private insurance company. Medicaid is coverage for health care that is provided by the government. It's best to check with your caseworker to find out about specifics that apply to your home state. Once you have applied for Medicaid, you will have a card with a number that allows you to receive medical services when presented at hospitals or clinics. Make sure you hold onto this card. It's a good idea to write down the number and keep it somewhere safe. Your caregivers and social workers should also have a copy of the card in case it is misplaced or lost.

When Can I See My Birth Parents?

Your relationship with your birth parents or any birth siblings really depends on your particular situation. Generally, you are entitled to meet with your birth parents as long as your caseworker and social worker do not believe that doing so will be harmful to you in any way. These visits may take place at your foster agency, or you might get permission to visit your birth parents on your own for a limited amount of time. The best thing to do is to ask your caseworker about this, as the rules vary depending on the state in which you live. However, if for any reason you have not been permitted to have these visits and your caseworker is not offering a lot of assistance, contact your caseworker's supervisor or speak up in court the next time you meet there.

What If I'm Not Comfortable with My Foster Family?

In 2001, the U.S. Congress passed legislation called the No Child Left Behind Act. Part of this law gave more rights to foster youth in need of permanent homes. Instead of placing youth with just any available family, agencies must now first try to recruit foster and adoptive families from communities that reflect the background of those needing new homes. This means you have a right to—and your agency must help you find—a home where you'll feel the most comfortable in terms of the language(s) that you speak, your ethnicity, and your race. In light of the fact that this may not always work out perfectly (you may have different religious beliefs than your caregivers), it's important for teens to know that if, for these reasons, you're not comfortable in a placement home, you have a legal right to speak up.

What About My Future?

Aside from having a voice in your day-to-day life, you have the right to be involved in creating a plan for the future. In the foster care system, this is called a service plan review (SPR), or sometimes a "family team meeting." SPRs are meetings held every six months that you will attend with your caseworker and your lawyer. From the age of ten onward, you should be invited to all of these meetings in order to discuss your future plans and work on a permanency planning goal, commonly referred to as a PPG. To help you make the most of your participation in these meetings, you may want to start thinking about some questions, like what are the steps needed to reach future goals? For example, if you think you'll want to go to college, you'll want to start looking into any federal, state, or private grants or loans.

Regardless of your goal (returning to a birth parent; being placed for adoption with a foster family or individual; being cared for by a permanency guardian; placement with a fit and willing relative; or identifying and having access to a permanent family connection), once you are fourteen, you should start receiving services that will help you transition to adulthood and living on your own. Other options that may be better suited to you include living with relatives, being adopted by foster parents, and living on your own or with another teenager in a subsidized apartment.

four

HOW DO I COPE WITH SO MUCH CHANGE?

When asked about the biggest challenge confronting foster youth, most teens in foster care refer to the difficulties in coping with so much change. As pointed out in the previous chapter, the average person in foster care moves around a fair bit. Along with each new placement comes a slew of new situations and new faces.

You may find that you react in many different ways to all these changes. Some teens find it fun and exciting to meet other foster teens, whether in a group home, treatment facility, or foster home where they can interact and forge bonds. At the same time, it's also very natural to feel overwhelmed or scared by change. If you're shy or introverted, it might be difficult for you to deal with so many new and different people, whether other teens or adults. You may have trouble opening up to or trusting people. Hopefully, even if you move homes, you'll often

Grief can be a very confusing and painful emotion to experience. If you feel that your sadness is getting to be too much, don't be afraid to speak up to your caseworker or someone else you can trust.

have the same caseworker to rely upon. However, in some cases, depending on where you are placed, this isn't always possible. The same goes for other adults you count on, such as teachers, social workers, and primary care physicians.

Coping with Grief

Moving is difficult under any circumstances, and for foster youth, it can be especially challenging. Aside from being nervous or anxious, you'll likely feel extremely sad. This sadness can be magnified if you have just left or been taken from the home of your birth parents. Everyone experiences emotions differently. You may be aware of these feelings right away or you may have what is called a delayed reaction, in which the reality of your situation doesn't hit home until days, weeks, or even months later.

This sense of sadness and loss can come out in different ways. Some teens retreat inside themselves, steering clear of others and wanting only to be alone. Others feel angry. They might be rude or hostile to those around them, even if they don't mean to be. In general, adults in the foster care system are sensitive to what you're going through. Although they may not have experienced it firsthand, they have received training and have come into contact with other foster children. They understand that having to leave your home and family means saying good-bye (hopefully temporarily) to a lot of people who are extremely important to you. Sometimes, caseworkers are able to place teens close to their home, in some cases in the same

Instead of keeping your feelings bottled up inside, try to share the changes you're going through with your close friends. Having the support of someone who cares about you can help.

neighborhood. More often than not, however, you'll be placed in a home outside your community. What's tough about this is not only leaving your family and home, but also your neighborhood, school, and friends, as well as other important social ties such as a house of worship, sports team, club, community center, or even a part-time job.

To help deal with transitions and cope with grief and loss, you may want to speak with a counselor who is specially trained. It's also been found that writing about your feelings and experiences can be very soothing. You may want to keep a journal and write down your thoughts—as a poem, with drawings and sketches, as a story, or simply as an account of how you feel. Remember that keeping everything inside can sometimes make things seem overwhelming. There are also groups you can attend (ask your guidance counselor or social worker) where you meet and talk with other youth in the child welfare system.

Can I See My Birth Parents?

The amount of contact you have with your birth parents and siblings depends on many factors. Visiting rights are accorded on a case-by-case basis that takes into consideration each family's situation. Your caseworkers and caregivers want to help you stay in contact with your birth family, but sometimes circumstances such as illness, drug or alcohol addiction, or inaccurate contact information get in the way. Also, a lot of the visits may take place in the agency, which means you may have only a limited amount of time with your parents or siblings, in surroundings that don't feel very homelike. There are other times when it may be difficult to make it on time to these visits. Appointments can get delayed due to traffic, transportation, and weather problems, as well as last-minute changes in scheduling.

Before visiting with your birth family, you should prepare yourself emotionally. Due to everything they have been through, it's very normal for foster teens to have mixed feelings about

Lindsey Cherry holds up a photo of her siblings taken in Indianapolis, Indiana. Cherry doesn't know much about her siblings because they were split up after they entered foster care.

their birth parents. If you entered foster care when you were an infant or toddler, you may have very limited memories of your birth parents. It's hard to say whether or not this makes things easier or harder; it really depends on your unique circumstances. While loving and missing your parents, you may also feel angry or resentful toward them. You may feel that they let you down or they don't care about you.

You will probably go through phases where you experience some or all of these feelings. You may not even understand some of the feelings you have or why you have them. Your best option is to talk it out. You should know that you have access to therapists or social workers who are specially trained to help foster youth cope with their emotional pain. It's also useful to check with your caseworker to see if there are any professionally run support groups you can attend.

Perhaps you can relate to some of the following questions foster youth commonly ask themselves: Did I do something wrong? Was it my fault that I was taken away from my parents? Did I contribute to the breakdown of their marriage or their drug or alcohol abuse? Wasn't I good enough for them? I love them and they love me so why can't we live together?

These are tough questions, and you may find it difficult to accept, but the fact is that you didn't do anything wrong. Adults are humans, too, and sometimes they make mistakes. At times, their own personal problems may get in the way of them being good parents. There may be periods where you are not able to live together in a healthy environment. This can be the case if your parents are struggling with drug and alcohol abuse, with severe illnesses that require a lot of special care, or with difficult conditions such as joblessness or homelessness. Under such circumstances, even with all of the love in the world, it can become extremely hard to manage day-to-day life.

Remember that the ultimate goal of the child welfare system is to ensure that every young person leaves the system with a permanent family connection.

What About My Siblings?

An equally difficult part of being in foster care is the possibility of being separated from your brothers and sisters. Increasingly, child welfare experts say that, in most cases, siblings should be able to stay connected during foster care. That means trying to have siblings placed or eventually adopted into the same family. If it's not possible for you to be placed with your brother(s) and/or sister(s), your agency should set up sibling visits and cover transportation costs so that you can keep in touch. If that's not happening, tell your lawyer (and the judge at your next permanency hearing). Also, make a plan with your siblings for staying in touch.

Chapter five

WHAT HAPPENS WHEN I GROW TOO OLD FOR FOSTER CARE?

Teens must remain in foster care until they reach adulthood (eighteen years of age). However, most people choose to remain in foster care until they turn twenty-one. This is possible if, upon turning eighteen, you sign a consent document stating that you want to stay in the foster care system and you are enrolled in a school or a technical training program. Those who lack the skills or ability to live independently can also remain in foster care until the age of twenty-one.

Foster teens and adults between the ages of eighteen and twenty-one will continue to attend permanency hearings. At this point, these meetings are really important. "Aging out"—the term used to describe the transition from foster care to independent living—is more than just another big change. It's the most

Eighteen-year-old Chanel Finley smiles in her new bedroom at Mi Casa, a home for former foster youth who are transitioning to independent living.

important step you'll take in becoming an adult and learning to live on your own. Knowing your options and being prepared is vital.

What Can I Do to Prepare?

Aside from participating in the permanency meetings and working together with your agency and lawyer, there are many other things you can do to help prepare for your future. No matter what your permanency goal is, starting at age fourteen, you should be attending life skills classes that cover many practical issues you'll later be confronted with. Remember, these classes are mandatory and you do receive a stipend for attending. These are some of the topics that should be covered:

- Managing at home
- Looking for housing
- Making and following a budget
- Discussing and working on skills needed for employment
- Problem-solving skills
- Career planning
- Health and wellness
- Finding support in the community or via the Internet

Permanency Planning

As you know, every young person in foster care has a permanency plan that outlines how you will live when you age out of foster care. Hopefully, you have already been working on your permanency goal for quite some time. If not, now is the time to get cracking—especially if you're an older teen. Go over your future options with your caseworker and your lawyer and make sure you go to all permanency meetings. After working together to decide on your goal, you, your agency, and your lawyer will present the plan to the family court judge who is responsible for going over the case. Make sure the goal represents what you want, and if you have any uncertainties, voice your concerns. Remember, this is your future.

Returning to Your Birth Parents

Once your parents have received help for serious illnesses or problems that prevented them from taking care of you, and they are willing and able to resume their parenting tasks, it's possible to return home to live with them providing that your caseworker and the family court agree on their fitness as guardians. Of course, this is wonderful news. Try to keep in mind, however, that even though they're your family, "going home" will be different. Things will likely have changed since you have been in foster care (usually, for the better; otherwise, you wouldn't be going home). You may be surprised to find that you don't actually feel "at home" right away. Things may feel a little strange at first and both you and your parents may be kind of nervous or awkward. Be prepared to take some time to adjust.

Being Adopted

Some foster teens' permanent goal is to be adopted—either by current foster parents, a previous foster family, or another adult they trust and love. If you are fourteen or older, you must give your consent to be adopted. No one can force you into a family against your will. However, you should also be aware that even if you have decided against adoption in the past,

Especially for those who have been in the foster care system for a long time, being adopted is a huge and wonderful step.

your caseworker might continue to talk to you about it in case you change your mind. It's not that your caseworker is being pushy, but he or she really wants to make certain that if you decide not to return home, you have a good, safe, permanent home.

There are some big differences between remaining in a foster home and being adopted. First, your adoptive parents will be legally responsible for you instead of the foster care agency. For this reason, before you go through with the adoption make sure you've sat down with your prospective parents and talked about major life issues that concern you. Having good communication and sharing values and points of view is important so that major conflicts don't crop up down the line. What do your parents expect from you and what do you expect from them? Even if your new parents receive an adoption subsidy or financial assistance, they are now fully responsible for

After attending an appointment at the Department of Housing to apply for subsidized housing, Shakhina Bellamy *(right)* gets a big hug from her social worker Johnnymae Gales.

any financial needs you may have such as clothing, school supplies, an allowance, and costs for any extracurricular activities. Make sure to communicate if you feel you are not getting what you need.

Of course, the biggest change of all is that, legally, you will have a new mother and father. This doesn't mean that you still can't have feelings for your birth parents or that they no longer have feelings for you. Having two sets of parents can be a little complicated. However, even if they have conflicted feelings about your adoption, your birth parents will probably be relieved that you are living with adults who not only care about you, but who are also able to look after you. In the end, the most important thing is that you have a good, safe home. Although it may be weird not to be with your birth parents, sometimes things happen in life that change the way you think things are supposed to be.

Independent Living

In the family court system, a foster teen's choice to live on his or her own is often referred to as "another planned living arrangement with a permanency resource," or APPLA for short. In most cases, your caseworker will also help you identify and work on a relationship with an adult who you really like, respect, and get along with. This person won't have legal custody but should be willing to be there for you when you need help. You'll want it to be someone whom you can rely on to give you useful advice and emotional support as you make the transition from foster care to being self-sufficient. It could be a teacher, an older sibling, or a caseworker with whom you've developed a strong bond. Whoever it is, he or she should be like a mentor or trusted advisor to you. To ensure that this person is a good choice, your case will be discussed in family court.

There are a lot of people out there who want to help and who are willing to share their time, experience, and knowledge with teenagers in the foster care system. Be thankful for their guidance, do your best, and maybe later you will become a mentor to other foster teens.

aging out The common term used to refer to young people reaching the age of leaving foster care.

APPLA (another planned permanent living arrangement) The goal for a young person who is aging out of foster care and plans to live on his or her own. APPLA is also referred to as a goal of independent living.

AWOL (absent without leave) The term used for foster youth who leave placement without permission from the agency.

consent To agree, or give permission.

delayed Put off until a later time.

deny To refuse to agree.

empower To give power or strength.

group home A group living arrangement for young people in foster care who go to work or school in the community. Group homes are staffed by foster care workers.

introverted To be shy or reserved.

legislation A law or multiple laws that are created and put into action.

minor The legal term used to describe youth under the age of eighteen.

permanency plan goal (PPG) The best option for a permanent living situation once a foster youth ages out of care.

permanency plan review The family court review of a foster care agency. A permanency hearing is held every six months.

residential treatment center (RTC) A group living arrangement for young people in foster care who receive therapeutic services, education, and housing while living in a structured campus setting.

service plan review A meeting held every six months that foster youth attend with their caseworker and lawyer to discuss their future permanency plan.

Annie E. Casey Foundation
701 St. Paul Street
Baltimore, MD 21202
(410) 547-6600
Web site: http://www.aecf.org
  This foundation makes grants for vulnerable youth and
  their families.

Child Welfare Information Gateway
U.S. Department of Health and Human Services
200 Independence Avenue SW
Washington, DC 20201
(877) 696-6775
Web site: http://www.childwelfare.gov
  As part of the Children's Bureau, Administration for
  Children and Families, the Information Gateway promotes
  the well-being of foster youth by connecting child welfare,
  adoption, and related professionals to vital information.

Child Welfare League of America
440 First Street NW, 3rd Floor
Washington, DC 20001-2085
(202) 638-2952
Web site: http://www.cwla.org

This organization is comprised of hundreds of public and private organizations and agencies that are devoted to the safety, permanency, and well-being of all children and youth in the United States.

Dave Thomas Foundation: Finding Forever Families for
    Children in Foster Care
525 Metro Place North, Suite 220
Dublin, OH 43017
(800) 275 3832
Web site: http://www.davethomasfoundation.org
    This is a nonprofit organization and public charity dedicated
    to supporting adoptions of youth in foster care in North
    America. It was created by Wendy's restaurant founder Dave
    Thomas, who was adopted as a child.

Foster Care Youth United
Youth Communications
224 West 29th Street, 2nd Floor
New York, NY 10001
(212) 279-0708
Web site: http://www.youthcomm.org
    A great resource for youth in foster care, this association also
    publishes *Represent* magazine, written by and for teenagers
    in the foster care system.

HUD Resources for Youth
Leaving Foster Care

U.S. Department of Housing and Urban Development

451 7th Street SW

Washington, DC 20410

(202) 708-1112

Web site: http//www.hud.gov

   This service provides housing assistance to teenagers who are aging out of foster care.

North American Council on Adoptable Children (NACAC)

970 Raymond Avenue, Suite 106

St. Paul, MN 55114

(651) 644-3036

Web site: http://www.nacac.org

   This organization promotes and supports permanent families for youth in the foster care system in the United States and Canada.

Office of the Children's Lawyer

Ministry of the Attorney General

McMurtry-Scott Building

720 Bay Street, 11th Floor

Toronto, ON M5G 2K1

Canada

(800) 518-7901

Web site: http://www.attorneygeneral.jus.gov.on.ca

   The Office of the Children's Lawyer is a law office in the Ministry of the Attorney General that "delivers programs in the administration of justice on behalf of children under the age of eighteen with respect to their personal and property rights."

Web Sites

Due to the changing nature of Internet links, Rosen Publishing has developed an online list of Web sites related to the subject of this book. This site is updated regularly. Please use this link to access the list:

http://www.rosenlinks.com/faq/fost

For Further Reading

Eldridge, Sherrie. *Twenty Things Adopted Kids Wish Their Adoptive Parents Knew*. New York, NY: Delta, 1999.

Hazen, Lynn E. *Shifty*. Berkeley, CA: Tricycle Press, 2008.

Herlem, Fanny Cohen. *Great Answers to Difficult Questions About Adoption: What Children Need to Know*. London, England: Jessica Kingsley Publishers, 2008.

Krebs, Betsy. *Beyond the Foster Care System: The Future for Teens*. Rutgers University Press. New Brunswick: NJ, 2006.

Pelzer, Richard B. *A Teenager's Journey: Overcoming a Childhood of Abuse*. New York, NY: Warner Books, 2006.

Schein, Elyse. *Identical Strangers: A Memoir of Twins Separated and Reunited*. New York, NY: Random House, 2008.

Shirk, Martha. *On Their Own: What Happens to Kids When They Age Out of the Foster Care System*. New York, NY: Basic Books, 2006.

Silverstein, Deborah N. *Siblings in Adoption and Foster Care: Traumatic Separations and Honored Connections*. Santa Barbara, CA: Praeger Publishers, 2008.

Toth, Jennifer. *Orphans of the Living: Stories of America's Children in Foster Care*. New York, NY: Touchstone Press, 1998.

Index

About the Author

Annie Leah Sommers is an editor and writer. She has a B.A. in English literature from McGill University, an M.A. in children's literature from the Center for the Study of Children's Literature at Simmons College, and a diploma in secondary English and E.S.L. (English as a second language) from McGill University in Montreal.

Photo Credits

Cover © www.istockphoto.com/Loretta Hostettler; pp. 6, 10, 15, 34, 43, 50–51, 52 AP Images; p. 8 © Paul Kitagaki Jr./ Sacramento Bee/ZUMA Press; p. 18 © www.istockphoto.com/ Nancy Catherine Walker; p. 21 David Young-Wolff/Riser/Getty Images; p. 23 © www.istockphoto.com/asiseeit; p. 29 © Jose M. Osorio/Sacramento Bee/ZUMA Press; p. 31 Melanie Stetson Freeman/Christian Science Monitor/Getty Images; p. 39 © www. istockphoto.com/Joselito Briones; p. 41 © www.istockphoto.com/ Galina Barskaya; p. 47 © Bob Pepping/Contra Costa Times/ ZUMA Press.

Designer: Nicole Russo; Editor: Nicholas Croce;
Photo Researcher: Amy Feinberg